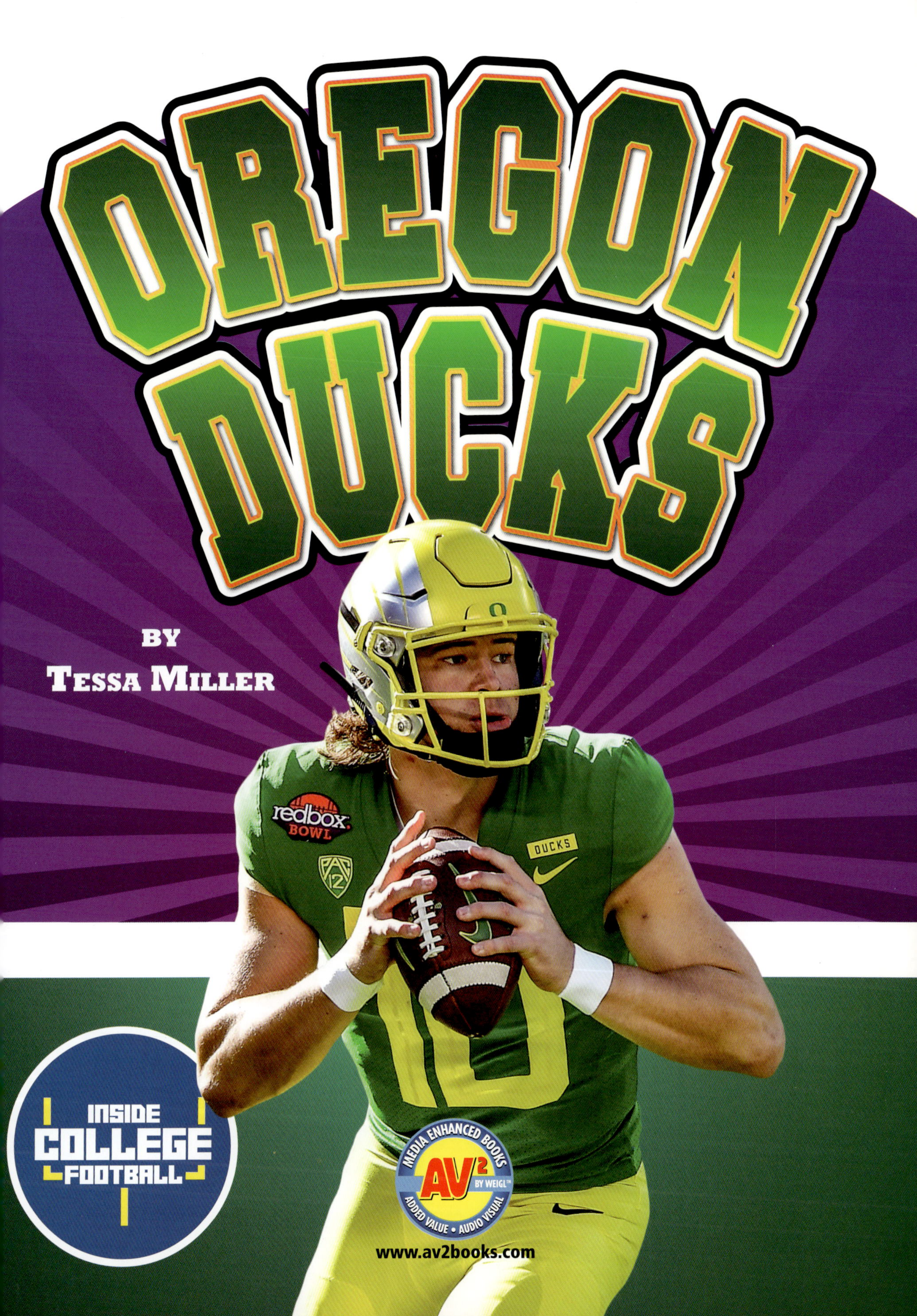
OREGON
DUCKS
BY
TESSA MILLER
redbox BOWL
DUCKS
INSIDE
COLLEGE
FOOTBALL
MEDIA ENHANCED BOOKS
AV2
BY WEIGL
ADDED VALUE • AUDIO VISUAL
www.av2books.com

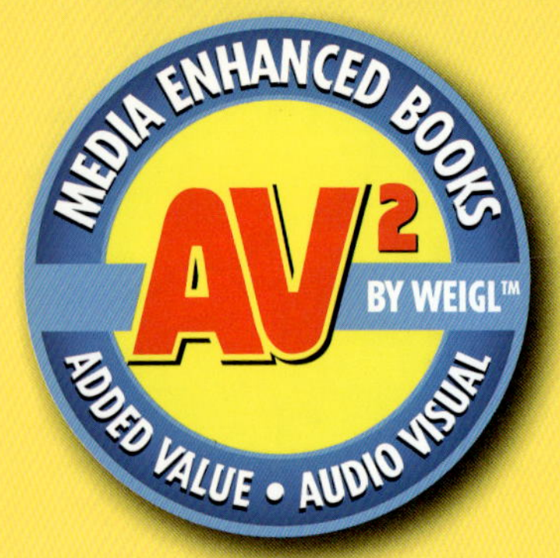

Go to www.av2books.com, and enter this book's unique code.

BOOK CODE

AVG88789

AV² by Weigl brings you media enhanced books that support active learning.

AV² provides enriched content that supplements and complements this book. Weigl's AV² books strive to create inspired learning and engage young minds in a total learning experience.

Your AV² Media Enhanced books come alive with...

Audio
Listen to sections of the book read aloud.

Video
Watch informative video clips.

Embedded Weblinks
Gain additional information for research.

Try This!
Complete activities and hands-on experiments.

Key Words
Study vocabulary, and complete a matching word activity.

Quizzes
Test your knowledge.

Slideshow
View images and captions, and prepare a presentation.

... and much, much more!

Published by AV² by Weigl
350 5th Avenue, 59th Floor
New York, NY 10118
Website: www.av2books.com

Library of Congress Control Number: 2018968215

ISBN 978-1-7911-0108-4 (hardcover)
ISBN 978-1-7911-0109-1 (multi-user eBook)
ISBN 978-1-7911-0110-7 (single-user eBook)

Printed in Guangzhou, China
1 2 3 4 5 6 7 8 9 0 23 22 21 20 19

042019
102318

Project Coordinator: Jared Siemens   Designer: Terry Paulhus

Every reasonable effort has been made to trace ownership and to obtain permission to reprint copyright material. The publishers would be pleased to have any errors or omissions brought to their attention so that they may be corrected in subsequent printings.

The publisher acknowledges Alamy, Getty Images, and Wikimedia Commons as its primary image suppliers for this title.

Oregon Ducks

CONTENTS

Introduction

The Oregon Ducks play for the University of Oregon in Eugene, Oregon. Eugene is best known in the sports world as the home of **Nike**. The University of Oregon is well known for its stellar **track and field** teams and has earned the nickname "Track Town, USA." However, its football team is also gaining national recognition.

The Ducks play in the Division I conference and are a member of the Pacific-12 (Pac-12) Conference, which was previously called the Pacific-10 (Pac-10) Conference. The first Oregon Ducks football team took the field in 1894. Many coaches led the Ducks during the program's first several decades. The team struggled during these years, with only a handful of winning seasons and national rankings. The football program became well known in the mid-1990s under the leadership of Mike Bellotti. The Ducks are still known for the **offensive** game Bellotti brought to the team during his time as head coach.

Oregon running back CJ Verdell logged 1,333 total yards and scored 12 touchdowns during the 2018 season.

Oregon has made a name for itself in the Pac-12 in recent years, with six conference championships since 2000. Ducks players continue to be among the most popular recruits to National Football League (NFL) teams. Their offensive line is strong, and veteran players on the line make the future bright for the Ducks.

Wide receiver Dillon Mitchell finished the 2018 season with 1,184 receiving yards for the Ducks. Mitchell's total was the highest in the Pac-12, and marked Oregon's 11th 1,000-yard receiving season in team history.

O

OREGON

Stadium Autzen Stadium

Division Pacific-12 (Pac-12) North

Head Coach Mario Cristobal

Location Eugene, Oregon

National Championships 0

Nicknames Ducks, Webfoots

227 Players Drafted into the NFL/AFL

11 Conference Championships

4 Pac-12 North Division Titles

101 Seasons Played

History

The 1983 **Civil War** game was played in the rain and ended in a **0–0 tie.**

Running back Taj Griffin had 9 carries, 65 rushing yards, and a touchdown in Oregon's victory over Oregon State in the 2015 Civil War game.

The Ducks played their first football game on March 24, 1894. That year, coaching duties were handled by two coaches, Cal Young and J.A. Church. For the first five years, the football team never left the state to face **rivals**. Finally, in 1899, the Ducks traveled to Berkeley, California, where they played the University of California Golden Bears.

The Ducks' biggest rivals are the University of Washington Huskies and the Oregon State University Beavers. Every year since 1894, the two Oregon teams end the regular season by playing each other in an **annual** rivalry game called the Civil War. This rivalry is the seventh-oldest football rivalry in the United States. The two schools are only 50 miles (80 kilometers) apart. This gives fans from both schools a unique opportunity to attend the game. The Civil War game has been played 122 times. The Ducks lead the series over the Beavers 65–47–10. Recently, they won in 2018, beating Oregon State 55–15.

The Ducks' recent seasons have been mostly successful. The veteran offensive line is once again leading the team forward. Oregon ended the 2017 season placed fourth in the Pac-12 North Division. The Ducks also played in the Las Vegas Bowl, where they were defeated by the Boise State University Broncos.

In their inaugural game, the Ducks defeated the Albany College Pioneers, now called the Lewis and Clark College Pioneers, 44–2.

The Stadium

The old artificial turf at Autzen Stadium was removed and replaced with newer FieldTurf in 2010. The field, which was slightly sloped to assist with drainage, was also leveled during the turf replacement.

The Ducks play all their home games in Autzen Stadium. Built in 1966, the stadium holds 54,000 seated fans with room for up to 600 standing fans. The stadium only took nine months to build and cost the university $2.5 million.

In 2002, Autzen underwent a **renovation** that cost the university $80 million. It added thousands of seats and luxury boxes for fans. It was the most costly renovation to date. The most recent renovations to Autzen were in 2014. Digital screens were added to the scoreboards and additional TV monitors were added to the concession areas. This way, fans never miss out on any of the action.

Autzen has a sunken field, which lets fans be closer to the action. This also means that the fan noise is extremely loud. Fans and coaches call the **reverberations** of the fans the "Autzen Bounce." Although the Ducks lost their first game in Autzen Stadium, they have enjoyed many winning seasons there in recent years. Record attendance for the stadium was set on October 15, 2011, when 60,055 fans gathered to watch the Ducks take on Arizona State University.

"DuckVision" was installed in 2008. The high-definition LED video board displays the score and allows fans to see replays of some of the game's most exciting moments.

Where They Play

Welcome to Autzen Stadium, home of the University of Oregon Ducks. Fans regularly exceed Autzen's capacity, filling the stands with a display of yellow and green. The noise of the crowd makes the ground shake as the team takes the field. The Ducks are ready to play.

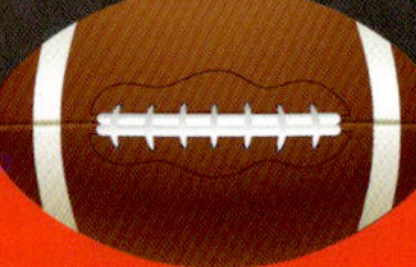

PAC-12 NORTH

1. **Oregon State University**
   Corvallis, Oregon
2. **Stanford University**
   Stanford, California
3. **University of California**
   Berkeley, California
4. ★ **University of Oregon**
   Eugene, Oregon
5. **University of Washington**
   Seattle, Washington
6. **Washington State University**
   Pullman, Washington

Arena
Autzen Stadium

Location
Eugene, Oregon

Broke Ground
1966

Completed
1967

Surface
Artificial Turf

Features
- Largest sports arena in the state of Oregon
- Fans' cheers were recorded at 127.2 decibels on October 27, 2007
- High-definition 33-by-85-foot (10-by-26-meter) video board

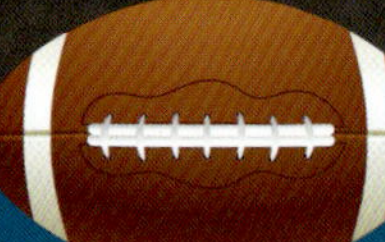

PAC-12 SOUTH

1. **Arizona State University**
   Tempe, Arizona
2. **University of Arizona**
   Tucson, Arizona
3. **University of California, Los Angeles**
   Los Angeles, California
4. **University of Colorado Boulder**
   Boulder, Colorado
5. **University of Southern California**
   Los Angeles, California
6. **University of Utah**
   Salt Lake City, Utah

WASHINGTON
OREGON
IDAHO
MONTANA
NORTH DAKOTA
SOUTH DAKOTA
MINNESOTA
WISCONSIN
WYOMING
IOWA
NEBRASKA
NEVADA
UTAH
COLORADO
KANSAS
MISSOURI
CALIFORNIA
ARIZONA
NEW MEXICO
OKLAHOMA
ARKANSAS
TEXAS
LOUISIANA
Pacific Ocean
1
2
3
4
5
6
1
2
3
4
5
6
N
S
E
W
SCALE
0 miles
500 miles
0 kilometers
500 km
LEGEND
Home Stadium
Pac-12 North
Pac-12 South
United States
Other Countries
Water

The Uniforms

Before the **2018** season began, Oregon announced the color combinations for **every game** so that fans could match the players on game days.

Before Oregon's partnership with Nike, the Ducks wore some of college football's most traditional uniforms. Today, Oregon takes the field in unique colors and designs, including several variations of duck feathers on the chest and shoulders of the jersey.

The Oregon Ducks are known for their constantly changing uniforms. In the 2011 season alone, they wore 12 different uniform combinations. The school's colors are officially green and yellow, but they also have black uniforms. One reason the Ducks can change gear so often is their partnership with Nike.

HOME

The Nike company has had the rights to the Ducks' uniforms since 1995. Before this partnership, the Ducks' uniforms were very traditional. They were a simple combination of yellow and green with yellow helmets. Today, the uniforms change every game, from socks to helmet designs. The team is also known for changing uniforms to support various causes. On October 19, 2013, the team sported pink helmets and bright pink shoes to support breast cancer awareness.

AWAY

The original **logo**, an interlocking "UO," was first added to the uniforms in 1977 by Coach Rich Brooks. However, Nike changed the logo in 1999 to its current look, which is a green or yellow "O." Their stylish and ever-changing uniforms keep the team on the cutting edge of football uniform style.

While many teams have worn pink socks or pink ribbon helmet stickers during Breast Cancer Awareness Month, Oregon has made a bold statement with hot pink helmets.

Student Athletes

Oregon student athletes have achieved an **80 percent graduation rate** for the past seven years, an all-time high for the university.

The Ducks are the 12th most valuable college football team in America, and the most valuable team in the Pac-12 Conference. The team makes an average of $92 million in revenue and $54 million in profit every year.

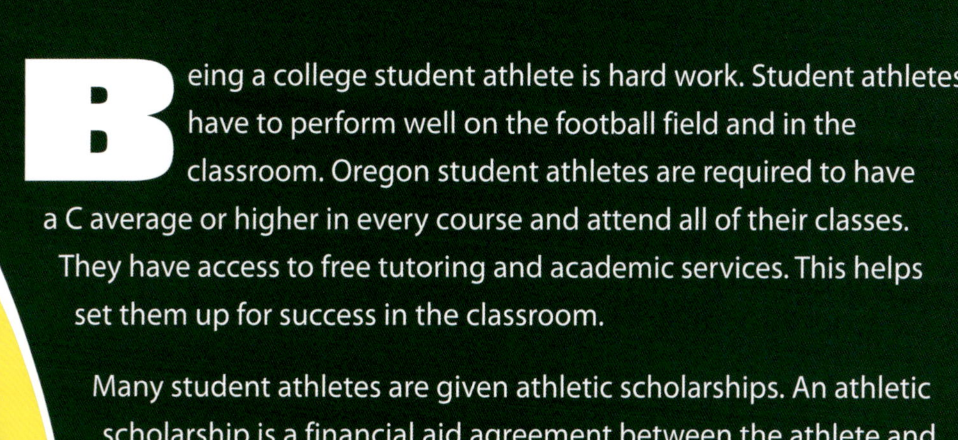

Being a college student athlete is hard work. Student athletes have to perform well on the football field and in the classroom. Oregon student athletes are required to have a C average or higher in every course and attend all of their classes. They have access to free tutoring and academic services. This helps set them up for success in the classroom.

Many student athletes are given athletic scholarships. An athletic scholarship is a financial aid agreement between the athlete and the college or university. Athletes who do not receive an athletic scholarship can also be "walk-on" members of the team. This means they are on the team, but without athletic financial aid. Oregon awards the maximum number of football scholarships allowed, which is 85. Oregon also provides full medical care for athletes during their time at the university.

Freshman student athletes such as Penei Sewell are able to attend tutoring and advising sessions in a special area of the John E. Jaqua Academic Center for Student Athletes called "Frosh Hall."

Bowl Games

The Ducks have won three of the seven Rose Bowl Games they have played in.

The Rose Bowl Game trophy is officially known as the Leishman Trophy, and is named for William Leishman, who led the construction of the Rose Bowl. The Ducks won the Leishman Trophy in 2015 with the help of Heisman Memorial Trophy winner Marcus Mariota.

After the college football season ends, a rare sports tradition begins. There is no National Collegiate Athletic Association (NCAA)-sponsored **postseason** for the sport of football. Instead, a variety of games called bowl games are played. There are currently 40 bowl games played between college football teams. These games give teams the chance to play rivals or new teams. It is also a chance to compete for respect and wins even after teams have finished with the regular season.

Bowl games are not mandatory for players. Athletes with injuries or upcoming NFL **prospects** often opt out of playing in bowl games. For the Oregon Ducks, the Rose Bowl is considered the highest achievement, because it means they are at the top of the Pac-12. The Ducks have played in the Rose Bowl more than any other bowl, but they have played in many other bowls as well, including the Fiesta Bowl, the Alamo Bowl, and the Las Vegas Bowl. The Ducks have played in 32 bowl games and have won 14.

The Ducks' most recent bowl win was their 2018 defeat of Michigan State University in the Redbox Bowl. Oregon won the game by a single point.

The Coaches

Rich Brooks Field at Autzen Stadium is named after the team's **longest-serving** head coach.

Current head coach Mario Cristobal was Oregon's offensive line coach, co-offensive coordinator, and run game coordinator for most of the 2017 season. He was named head coach in December 2017.

The Oregon Ducks have had 34 head football coaches in their 101 seasons. The team's coaching got off to a rocky start. The Ducks' first head coach left after their very first game. Over the next 21 seasons, 18 different head coaches came and went. This turnover of coaches led to some rough patches for the team. However, some of the shortest-serving coaches have led the Ducks to some of their most successful seasons.

LEN CASANOVA Len Casanova coached the Ducks for 16 seasons from 1951 to 1966. In that time, he had an 82–73–8 record. He had eight winning seasons and is ranked third in the team's history for overall wins. In 1957, Casanova led the team to the Rose Bowl. After his time as head coach, Casanova served as the school's athletic director for four years.

MIKE BELLOTTI Mike Bellotti was the Ducks' coach from 1995 to 2008. During his 14 seasons, he led the Ducks to 116 wins. His record of 116 wins to 55 losses ranks him number-one in overall wins in the team's history. He also coached the team to two Pac-10 Conference championships. In 2001, the Ducks also won the conference title, the Fiesta Bowl, and finished second in the national rankings.

CHIP KELLY Even though Chip Kelly only coached the Ducks for four seasons, he is considered one of the team's best coaches. From 2009 to 2012, Kelly led the team to three winning seasons. His overall coaching record at Oregon was 46–7–0. In 2010, the Ducks ended the regular season undefeated. They also went 12–1 and won the Fiesta Bowl in the 2012 season.

The Mascot

The Duck does a pushup for every point on the board each time Oregon scores. Oregon has 39 games with 50 or more points since 2009, making The Duck one of college football's fittest mascots.

The mascot for the University of Oregon is a duck. In the 1920s, live ducks were brought to football and basketball games. The teams at the university called themselves the "Webfoots." Notably, one duck named Puddles became a fan favorite. However, live duck mascots were banned in the 1940s.

In 1947, a deal was struck between the athletic director of the university and the Walt Disney Company. The agreement allowed the team's mascot to be modeled after Disney's Donald Duck. The present mascot officially came into being in 1973. It is referred to simply as "The Duck." The Duck wears a green and yellow costume and a green beanie hat with "Oregon" across the front. In 2010, Disney released the University of Oregon from a licensing agreement that required their permission every time the mascot appeared. The release allows The Duck to attend more non-sporting events and compete in the mascot national championship.

Before each home game, The Duck is escorted into Autzen Stadium on the back of a custom-painted Oregon-themed Harley Davidson motorcycle.

Legends of the Past

For many players, their time with the Ducks is the start of a promising football career. These are some of the best-known football players to play for the University of Oregon.

Marcus Mariota

Marcus Mariota is considered the best quarterback the Ducks have ever had. He played from 2012 to 2014. As a freshman, he led the Ducks to a 12–1 record and a Fiesta Bowl victory. As a sophomore, he led the Ducks to an 11–2 record and an Alamo Bowl victory. During his junior year, Mariota became the first Oregon Duck to win the Heisman trophy and led the team to a Rose Bowl victory. Mariota was drafted after his junior year by the Tennessee Titans in the first round of the 2015 NFL **draft**.

Position: Quarterback
Seasons: 2012–2014 (Oregon Ducks), 2015–Present (Tennessee Titans)
Born: October 30, 1993, Honolulu, Hawai'i

LaMichael James

LaMichael James is the top-ranked running back of all time for the Oregon Ducks. During his three seasons at Oregon, the Ducks won three consecutive Pac-12 Conference championships. He also went to two Rose Bowls and a National Championship game. James is currently ranked second at Oregon for rushing yards, with 5,082, and for touchdowns, with 58. After his junior year, James was drafted by the San Francisco 49ers in the second round of the 2012 NFL draft.

Position: Running Back
Seasons: 2009–2011 (Oregon Ducks), 2012–2014 (San Francisco 49ers), 2014–2015 (Miami Dolphins)
Born: October 22, 1989, New Boston, Texas

Royce Freeman

Royce Freeman is the Ducks' most decorated player. He came to the Oregon Ducks in 2014 as the highest-ranked recruit that season. He had a very successful freshman year, which included being named Pac-12 Freshman Offensive Player of the Year. Freeman set multiple records during his time with the Ducks. He set an Oregon and Pac-12 record with 5,621 rushing yards. His 6,435 all-purpose yards are also an Oregon record. He carried the ball more than any other Duck player and scored a record 384 points. In 2018, the Denver Broncos chose Freeman in the third round of the NFL draft.

Position: Running Back
Seasons: 2014–2017 (Oregon Ducks), 2018–Present (Denver Broncos)
Born: February 24, 1996, Imperial, California

Joey Harrington

Joey Harrington is considered one of the best players in Ducks history. His father played for the University of Oregon, and when Joey was born, the head coach at the time sent him a letter of intent asking the infant to commit to playing football when he got into college. The early letter paid off. Harrington eventually led the team to its first-ever 11-game winning season. In 2001, he led the team to a win at the Fiesta Bowl. He left the Oregon Ducks with a 25–3 record. Harrington was drafted into the NFL in 2002 to play for the Detroit Lions, and he retired in 2008.

Position: Quarterback
Seasons: 1998–2001 (Oregon Ducks), 2002–2005 (Detroit Lions), 2006 (Miami Dolphins), 2007 (Atlanta Falcons), 2008 (New Orleans Saints)
Born: October 21, 1978, Portland, Oregon

All-Time Records

10,796

Career Passing Yards

Marcus Mariota holds Oregon's record for career passing yards, with 10,796.

178

Career Receptions

Samie Parker's 178 career receptions was a Ducks record set in 2003 and tied by Jeff Maehl in 2010.

136

Career Touchdowns

Marcus Mariota scored 136 touchdowns, more than any player in Oregon history.

60
Career Rushing Touchdowns

Royce Freeman scored a record 60 rushing touchdowns for the Ducks.

30
Career Sacks

Nick Reed's 30 career sacks is an Oregon record, and the fourth highest in Pac-12 history.

1894
The University of Oregon plays its first game on March 24. The head coach leaves the team after this game.

1919
The Oregon Webfoots win their first conference championship for the University of Oregon.

1900

1920

1940

1960

In 1917, Head Coach Hugo Bezdek leads Oregon to its first Rose Bowl win. Hugo Bezdek is only one of two coaches to lead the team to an undefeated season.

1947
Athletic director Leo Harris strikes a deal with Walt Disney to use a likeness of Donald Duck as the university's mascot.

1967
Autzen Stadium, which has come to be known as one of college football's loudest stadiums, opens and becomes the Ducks' official home.

The Future

The Oregon Ducks continue to build themselves as an offensive team. Under Head Coach Mario Cristobal, they hope to continue their strong offensive line. Returning quarterback Justin Herbert is on track to be one of the Ducks' best quarterbacks of all time. He has reached 3,000 passing yards faster than any other player in Ducks history. With these two men leading the team, its future is bright.

2018

Mario Cristobal leads the Ducks to a 9–4 season.

1995

The University of Oregon signs a deal with Nike to design the team uniforms. As a result, the Ducks get to try out the newest designs and innovations for football uniforms from Nike before anyone else.

In 2015, the Ducks win their third Rose Bowl.

1980 2000 2020

1994

Mike Bellotti is hired as head coach, a move many fans believe made the football team a national contender for the first time.

2012

The Ducks win the Rose Bowl. Before this victory over the University of Wisconsin Badgers, the Ducks had not won a Rose bowl in 95 years.

Write a Biography

Life Story

A person's life story can be the subject of a book. This kind of book is called a biography. Biographies often describe the lives of people who have achieved great success. These people may be alive today, or they may have lived many years ago. Reading a biography can help you learn more about a great person.

Get the Facts

Use this book, and research in the library and on the internet, to find out more about your favorite player. Learn as much about him as you can. What position does he play? What are his statistics in important categories? Has he set any records? Also, be sure to write down key events in the person's life. What was his childhood like? What has he accomplished off the field? Is there anything else that makes this person special or unusual?

Use the Concept Web

A concept web is a useful research tool. Read the questions in the concept web on the following page. Answer the questions in your notebook. Your answers will help you write a biography.

Concept Web

Adulthood
- Where does this individual currently reside?
- Does he have a family?

Your Opinion
- What did you learn from the books you read in your research?
- Would you suggest these books to others?
- Was anything missing from these books?

Accomplishments off the Field
- What is this person's life's work?
- Has he received awards or recognition for accomplishments?
- How have this person's accomplishments served others?

Childhood
- Where and when was this person born?
- Describe his parents, siblings, and friends.
- Did he grow up in unusual circumstances?

Write a Biography

Help and Obstacles
- Did this individual have a positive attitude?
- Did he receive help from others?
- Did this person have a mentor?
- Did this person face any hardships?
- If so, how were the hardships overcome?

Accomplishments on the Field
- What records does this person hold?
- What key games and plays have defined his career?
- What are his stats in categories important to his position?

Work and Preparation
- What was this person's education?
- What was his work experience?
- How does this person work?
- What is the process he uses?

Trivia Time

Take this quiz to test your knowledge of the Oregon Ducks. The answers are printed upside down under each question.

1 When did the University of Oregon play its first game?

A. March 24, 1894

2 What were teams at the University of Oregon originally called?

A. The Webfoots

3 Where is the University of Oregon located?

A. Eugene, Oregon

4 Who are the Ducks' biggest rivals?

A. The University of Washington Huskies and the Oregon State University Beavers

5 What is the name of the annual game between rivals Oregon and Oregon State?

A. The Civil War

6 In which year did the Ducks win their first Rose Bowl?

A. 1917

7 What is the name of the stadium where the Ducks play?

A. Autzen Stadium

8 Who was the first Ducks quarterback to win the Heisman trophy?

A. Marcus Mariota

9 What Oregon-based company makes the uniforms for the Oregon Ducks football team?

A. Nike

10 What famous cartoon character is the University of Oregon's mascot modeled after?

A. Disney's Donald Duck

Key Words

annual: something that occurs once a year

draft: an annual event where the NFL chooses college football players to be new team members

logo: a symbol that stands for a team or organization

Nike: a brand of athletic clothing that is primarily known for shoes

offensive: having to do with attacking the opposite team in order to score points

postseason: a sporting event that takes place after the end of the regular season

prospects: players who are likely to succeed in a sport at a high level

renovation: construction that works to improve or expand an older building

reverberations: the continuation of a sound

rivals: groups or individuals who compete toward the same objective or goal

track and field: a sport that includes contests of running, jumping, and throwing

Index

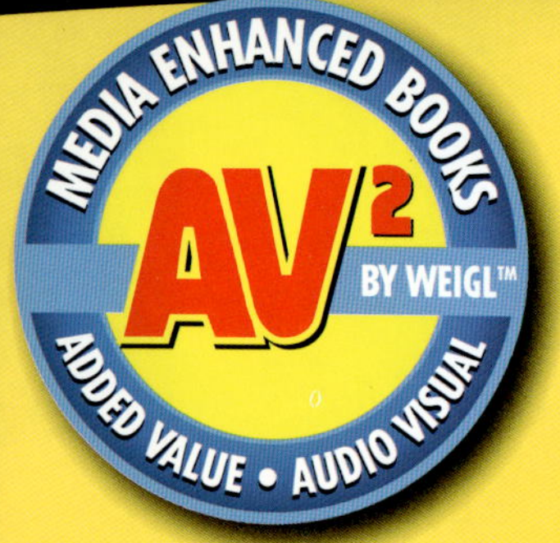

Log on to www.av2books.com

AV² by Weigl brings you media enhanced books that support active learning. Go to www.av2books.com, and enter the special code found on page 2 of this book. You will gain access to enriched and enhanced content that supplements and complements this book. Content includes video, audio, weblinks, quizzes, a slideshow, and activities.

AV² Online Navigation

Audio
Listen to sections of the book read aloud.

Book Pages
AV² pages directly correspond to pages in the book.

Video
Watch informative video clips.

Embedded Weblinks
Gain additional information for research.

Key Words
Study vocabulary, and complete a matching word activity.

Try This!
Complete activities and hands-on experiments.

Quizzes
Test your knowledge.

Slideshow
View images and captions, and prepare a presentation.

AV² was built to bridge the gap between print and digital. We encourage you to tell us what you like and what you want to see in the future.

Sign up to be an AV² Ambassador at www.av2books.com/ambassador.

Due to the dynamic nature of the internet, some of the URLs and activities provided as part of AV² by Weigl may have changed or ceased to exist. AV² by Weigl accepts no responsibility for any such changes. All media enhanced books are regularly monitored to update addresses and sites in a timely manner. Contact AV² by Weigl at 1-866-649-3445 or av2books@weigl.com with any questions, comments, or feedback.